John Brady McDonald

What Shade of Brown?

This book was originally written on a
1969 Commodore 4400 typewriter and a
1968 Remington Ten-Forty typewriter

John Brady McDonald

What Shade of Brown?

poetry

Editor: Jordy Ironstar
Cover art: John Brady McDonald
Book and cover design: Tania Wolk, Third Wolf Studio
Printed and bound in Canada at Friesens, Altona, MB

The publisher gratefully acknowledges the support of Creative Saskatchewan, the Canada Council for the Arts and SK Arts.

creative SASKATCHEWAN
Canada Council for the Arts Conseil des Arts du Canada
sk arts

Library and Archives Canada Cataloguing in Publication

Title: What shade of brown? / John Brady McDonald.
Other titles: What shade of brown? (Compilation)
Names: McDonald, John, 1981- author.
Identifiers: Canadiana 20250192632 | ISBN 9781998926282 (softcover)
Subjects: LCGFT: Poetry.
Classification: LCC PS8625.D6374 W43 2025 | DDC C811/.6—dc23s.ca

radiant press
Box 33128 Cathedral PO
Regina, SK S4T 7X2
info@radiantpress.ca

www.radiantpress.ca

Dedicated to the memory of
Victor Thunderchild,
Fred Sasakamoose,
and Karina Wolfe

Contents

Who Will Take the Candle

(The Night After the James Smith Massacre)

Who will take the candle into the darkness tonight?
Who will bring light to places we cannot see?
Who will stay with the Sacred Fire?
Who is even going to light it?
Perhaps we should all rest around it and make room
around the stones

I wish there were answers in my words
I wish my pen strokes could lift from this page
and turn into powerful medicine
I wish they would become an eagle-wing fan,
waving over us all

But I don't think these words can answer
Perhaps someone else's will

Away from the flames,
The Northern Lights have come to dance them all home

I Awoke to the Sound of Running Water

I awoke to the sound of running water
I looked up at the bathroom sink
The water trickled from old fashioned taps
Why was I on the bathroom floor?
It's a scary thing,
This unknowing

These things I am given in my sleep
Visions and images
Fear and hope
They make me walk in my sleep

When I pass the word along
They vanish from my mind
No longer needed
Purpose
Served
The slate wiped clean

There is an Odd Calm

There is an odd calm
In writing a poem on graph paper
Each letter in its own square
Like a poorly thought out
Crossword puzzle

No room for error
Each word locked in place
If you change your mind
You can't go back
You have to start again,
The whole thing
From the beginning
Literally
From Square One

Last Night I Had a Dream

I dreamed that I stood inside a roomful of books
It might have been a bookstore
It might have been a library
I'm not sure

Through the middle of this room
A great river flowed
It's waters dark green and blue

It flowed across the floor, not slowly
But not with great force, either
It was a strong current

I watched as people would come to the edge of the water
And cast lines into it

I watched as their lines grew taut with the current
As lines cast into rivers will do
Then I watched as their rods bent with each bite

I walked to the edge and looked into the water
Schools of books flowed back and forth like fish

I looked up and watched as the people reeled in book after book
Filling woven willow baskets at their feet
I gazed into the water again
And I saw my own books swimming back and forth
I smiled

But when I looked into the baskets on the shore,
I saw that my books were not in them

One by one, the people reeled in their lines
Picked up their baskets
And walked away

I looked down into the water
The pages of books, discarded like fish guts, were floating,
sopping wet, across the surface
I stood alone on the shore
The guts of books scattered at my feet

I remember as a starving child, dreaming of food
All the food I could eat
Dreaming of toys and treasures I never had

Knowing I was waking up, I would quickly clutch as
much of it as I could against my chest
Hoping it would still be there when I woke up

It still happens from time to time

I Look Out the Window

I look out the window to the south
Everything looks blue
Shaded and coloured a soft blue
The light of the day diffused by the clouds
And the swiftly falling snow blowing horizontal
Against the upright poplar trees across the field

The song, "Be My Baby"
On repeat in my head
Stuck there since Ronnie Spector died last week
The drum breakdown in the middle
Over and over

Hyper focused on the snow
Against the pickets of poplar trees
My mind a million miles away
Right now, stuck in a loop

The Humidity in the Air

the humidity in the air after a summer rain makes the paper
damp to the touch

it starts to curl, even before
I set it into the typewriter
And begin to roll it around the platen

Did you know that was what that part of a typewriter is called?
I didn't
I had to look it up

I stare out of an open window as I write this
The summer wind blowing the poplar and caragana leaves
While a crow yells into the sky, drowning out the songbirds

There is still the smell of summer rain in the wind
And the sky is grey between the leaves of my window
As the paper advances through this machine
It begins to curl the other way now

My Shoulders Were Once Light

My shoulders were once light
There was only the weight of my own life upon them
They did not bear the weight of the world
As they do now

I was young then
Blissfully unaware
Selfish as I was
In my own little world
With only my own troubles on my mind

My back is now stooped under it all
Bent like an old man
Groaning like an old wooden floor
Being walked upon again and again

I take the weight from my back
I use it to press down upon paper with my pen
Press down upon canvas with my brush
A pressure release before the boiler explodes

I'm bent in half you see
But I'm not broken in two

The Meeting

I didn't think that I would see them again.
It was shocking at first, but
the shock soon passed.

I felt a cold child between my shoulder blades, and
beneath my breath, I hid the words
"Oh, shit."

"Hello." they said, "You're looking good."

Funny, I thought. They said the same words
over a table of empty bottles
that night in Edmonton so long ago.

'Thanks," I said, "and so do you."

It was said in courtesy, if nothing else.
I clear my throat.
"So, how's it been?" I hear myself say,
but the rest of me really don't care.
I'm thinking of home and my new girl.

He begins to tell me of how their boyfriend is gone,
of how he left them on a Friday night at Charlie's.
He hasn't called.
"Asshole," they dub him.

Now they query me.
"So, how have YOU been?"

I notice that their eyes
are like the door in the Stone's song
red and painted black.
"Well," I begin,
choosing my words with care.
I don't want to hurt them, but
a lot has changed
since we shared that bed
in that hotel
in Edmonton.

Before I can continue, they speak up
and say, "I would've called you,
but I lost your number, and
before I could find it,
I met the asshole, and
well, you know..."

"Yeah, well, it happens,"
I tell them with a smile,
knowing full well
that the number I gave them
was the number
to a taxi stand in my hometown
because I was afraid to give them my real one.

"Listen, I gotta go," I say.
"It was good to see you!"
I turn to leave.

They call me back.

“Here, call me some time,”
They say,
and scribble their number
on a yellow slip of paper
from their pocket.

I swallow hard,
because I know that
I’m going to hurt them.
Christ, I can see it
in their eyes.

You’d swear I’d slapped them in the face
when I told them
I wouldn’t call.

They blinked once
or twice,
and then bit their bottom lip.

“Well,” they said,
“I didn’t know
you were with someone.
I guess I’ll
see you around.”
They turn and leave.

The sound of a teaspoon
stirring inside of
a coffee cup catches
my attention.

I could use a cup of coffee
right about now.

There's a tap on my shoulder.

"Hey, who was that?"
asks the voice of
my buddy who is buying me coffee
but doesn't know it yet.

"A guy I used to know,"
I reply,
and leave it at that.

We Are Surrounded by the Cold

We are surrounded by the cold at all times. It seems like winter still holds us like a jealous lover. Now would be a good time for a drive down a forgotten stretch of memory lane.

What's the matter, friend? Is it really the unknown holding you back? Are you really worried about that little leap of faith? C'mon, what's the worst that can happen to you, other than falling to your death?

Make do with what they gave you and be grateful that you were given anything at all. There are some out there who would love to have even a taste of what you have.

Read the words you need to read. If they don't exist, then write them. Sing the songs you need to sing. If they don't exist either, compose it. Remember that it is one thing to blow out a candle. Finding it in the darkness is another. Just stare out into the darkness for a little while. Who knows, you might just find the light.

I know it's been a while since we've felt exhaustion like this. Is this the calm before the storm, or is this the storm itself? Perhaps it's just the eye of the vortex, the middle of the road? Whatever it is, I'm tired too.

It's okay, I believe you. The gleaming gold that once was now lies tarnished at your feet. Your heart sits heavy within your chest, and your soul aches in your weary head. It's no fun meeting like this, and I know that you wish it would end, and, with your love, walk hand-in-hand away from this horrible feeling taking residence within you.
I know.

It has become so much trouble that it is no longer worth your precious time, and that anything here which served any real joy, has long ago fallen by the wayside. I see you wanting to walk away from the straight and narrow, with your love and your sanity intact, walk away from this fallen empire. If only it were that easy.

I see how pressure builds around you from those around us, goading you to stay on the path and maintain your word. I know that they beg you not to deviate. I can see it in your eyes. I can sense a question: “Why do I even bother?” You sit in constant scrutiny under innocent eyes, judged by those who should’ve witnessed what you are, not what you once were. Do they even know what it is you have become, immortalized and carved upon the coloured marble of history, set upon plinths of the past, to become the apples in the eyes of your keepers and well-wishers?

I see your dirty feet shackled; your feet bound to such a narrow and painful path. Do you see the road signs they have put up? A single step off this locked track is viewed with such horror, isn’t it? It is taboo, repulsive and grotesque, tantamount to an atrocity in the eyes of the innocents, and to those who would be your keepers. Ah, I feel for you, my friend. I really do. Christ, no wonder we are tired. I’m tired for you, and I am merely walking alongside, not shouldering the burden. I am no Good Samaritan, or whatever it was. I’m not carrying no cross, that’s not my bedtime story. I am but a wayward bumblebee, hovering around a single lightbulb along with the moths. It’s not my fate, but I will gladly share the time with you.

It’s strange how this mindset settled upon us all, isn’t it? How quickly it becomes ingrained into the mind and upon the heart. They are truly weak internal organs, despite their claims of superiority. They are far too susceptible to damage from stupid things.

If I were you, I would splash as much water as I could out of this fishbowl existence, where every word and every thought is collected and recorded, gassed within a killing jar, forced to inhale acetate before being pinned to a board like a beautiful butterfly, all in the name of the collective mind of those who hold themselves omnipotent and righteous.

I must hand it to you, my friend. It takes a strong mind to sit and be watched by the watchers; shattered, shuttered and confused, craving only your lover's sweet touch in the darkness.

There are those who will ask the same stupid questions, of course. They will ask, "Why does what they think matter so much to you?" They will wonder why you let it rattle you so. They cannot ask those questions of themselves, yet they expect you to answer them. The state of denial that grips them is simply beyond me. Where have they been all this time? Did they not see? We knew the truth of it all, no matter what they thought. They only see what they want to see anyway.

I hate to say it, friend, but one day, you may very well give up on giving a shit. I did, a long time ago, for a little while, at least. I proclaimed, "I do what I do for me, not for them. I have seen what I have seen and lived my life. Who are they to deny me my memories?"

Believe me, I know that I have asked too much of you, because you were the first to never hurt me. You were the only person I trusted with my emotions. I ran to you, I wanted to cling to you, not to own you or objectify you, but because I was an abused child, abandoned a long time ago, begging to be kept safe.

It was not the first time for me. I lost those first people, those kindred spirits, all good and gentle people, honest people. I still dream of them and of that place, once we stood, shoulder to shoulder, fighting the darkness and the devils out there, on the streets. I still dream of it often. You see, they were my family, closer than blood, bound and tied together by the fight and by the work, it was good work.

It's all gone now. The Rules of Engagement have been changed. The lights have been turned off. They have locked the doors with new locks, so our keys will not fit anymore. Perhaps they will tear that place down once and for all. The ties are cut now, and we have all drifted, like lifeboats from a sinking ship, still within our fields of vision, but growing miles apart with each gust of wind.

Yes, the drink was poisoned, and yes, the dancers suffered, but we too were dancers, dancing to music that always seemed slightly out of tune.

I hope that, when the lights were turned off one last time, although all these years have passed, someone had the sense to steal all the photos in the frames. Are we still just photos in a frame, or are we just an afterthought, of better times, of those days way back when?

The Steps You Take

The steps you take
May seem insignificant
Unless you stop and ask
If they are taken towards or away from
Where you need to be

Those that walk with their heads held high
Are often unaware of what they are stepping on

I keep my eyes on the ground
I watch my steps
So that I rarely stumble or step on anything

If I walk into anything though,
It's simply a matter of adjusting my steps

I Can Empathize

I can empathize with
The pain and angst
Frustration and retaliation
Born of deprivation and poverty
It was my world
I was cradled and swaddled by it
I know Hunger and Want

I cannot empathize
With attitudes and emotions
Born of privilege and wealth
I do not know this world
Nor understand the feelings born of
Greed and riches

When you say that you are not rich
You do not understand
For you have never known absolute hunger
Or have never wanted for anything

That itself is wealth beyond imagination to the hungry

In Another Life I Was a Hunter

In another life I was a hunter. I killed to eat. The setup is familiar, and the changes are slight, but it makes one more careful, that's all. It makes you concentrate just a little bit harder. It makes you take each step very carefully.

When the crack of the rifle echoes through quiet poplars, you exhale that breath you were only vaguely aware you were holding. The steam from your hot exhalation mingles with the muzzle smoke in the frigid air above your head. It is only then that you start to feel cold again, and you make your way down that long and lonely wooded hill, going to see if you are tracking the animal for a long way, or just the few yards it was able to make it before it ran itself out.

Pull apart these little moments and separate these days. Let the pull of your momentum guide you on your way. Do not let indecision cripple you. Let intention rest. Say what needs to be said. The energy caused by fear is a tumor upon the lungs of the earth.

Is it truly our destiny as what many of you still call Indians to die and become spirit guides for White psychics and spiritualists? No, you will not colonize me in death as you did in life.

Winter snows bow the spruce boughs low, the heavy weight of snow breaking evergreen limbs. The sharp crack echoes through the trees, amplified by the cold.

Winter always makes the senses sharper. I will gladly take sharpened wits over foolish words.

I do not belong out here, no matter what they say. I was not born into this winter. I was born into the altered climate of the city streets, where pavement and steel take the sun's heat and make the bite of the cold less than amongst the trees.
I think of cold, open water cutting your breath wide open. Jump into it, and you will gasp and open your eyes wide. It will force you to. You will do it involuntarily. Nature has its way of opening your eyes, once you are forced to, and she will force you, and you will be humbled, whether you like it or not. It is like you are pulled apart, torn into little strips of everything, and you won't even know where to begin. You'll be broken like a windowpane, open to the elements, letting the snow fly in.

Dear Darling One

for Jim

I

Dear darling one
It's been so long since I have sat at your table
Not since I was a much younger man,
when I used to sit almost at your feet
and would read with glee most willingly
the scraps of paper curled by your pen
and by the humidity
of the late summer evening
as they would roll off the table to
a hollow clatter to the floor

II

Thank you, but no
I no longer take the wine
It's been over twenty years since I've prayed
At the Altar of Dionysus
Those ways are not my ways anymore

III

You've been gone away for longer
Then you were ever here
Nearly three times as long

You were far younger than I am now

That's when I left your table,
When I crossed that threshold and became
Older than you would ever see

The rebellious idol becomes the foolish young person quickly
After the candles are blown out

IV
A brief visit, that's all
Just popping in for a quick hello for old times' sake
And to gather up my books,
The piles of them I left here the last time
When my travels took me in another direction

V
No, this isn't goodbye
I still love you

VI
My ride is waiting
It's time for me to go
It may be some time before I make my way here again

VII
I know that you don't have as many visitors
as you used to
But I'm sure there's still one or two
who keep you company.
I'll see you around sometime, OK?

I Came to the Sacred Fire

I came to the sacred fire as a young man
I should have been brought to it as a little boy
But I wasn't

I sought out the sacred fire on my own
I sought out the sacred fire to heal myself

I sought out the sacred fire to cleanse and burn away
The pain of a childhood rootless, without purpose
Filled with someone else's thoughts and prayers
and ways

I came to the sacred fire not as an empty vessel
to be filled
But as a dirty dish to be cleansed, scoured and rinsed of
the stains and muck
Of other peoples' bundles and pains

I sought out the sacred fire as someone
Lost in the night,
Cold and alone,
Wandering

The sacred fire welcomed me and made me warm
The sacred fire took the chill from my feet
and from my hands

I came to the sacred fire
And the teachings were given one at a time

I came to the sacred fire and the teachings were given
one at a time by brown, wrinkled hands
Far older than mine
They were hands that gave freely, for they knew I was listening

I sought out the sacred fire and was welcomed to it
By those who watched it taken away
Piece by piece, a long time ago

In the light of the sacred fire, I saw the grieving of a loss
I was just beginning to know

I step back from the sacred fire
I step back from the sacred fire,
not because I am afraid to burn

I step back from the sacred fire to watch the sparks
fly into the night

The Generation of Today

The generation of today
Unaware as they seem to be
Of the tyrants of the past
Their world a mass of noise
Blasting them from the palms of their hands

Water seeps through the cracks
It will always find its way
Taking the easiest route to earth
To the center of the earth
Gravitational pull

She pulled the book from the shelf
She stared at the cover for a long while
She asked me what it was
She asked me what she was to do with it

The older sister told her
That if it needed to be explained by now
She might as well just put it back

Do the children wander anymore?
Do they even wonder anymore?
Are they allowed?

The time has come to put down my brushes
The snow is melting
Mother Earth will do the painting now

Neither Servant nor Subservient

Neither servant nor subservient
We are never Less Than

Equal in care and affection to a child
We are partners in this nurturing of minds
Hand in glove
Through calm seas and chaos
Wiping tears and patting shoulders
Carrying home each night the worry
Fanning the spark until
It's ready to take

We are so much more than
Another set of eyes
Another set of hands
Another adult in the room

Day after day, we are fellow sculptors
in this sacred space
Sharing equally
Magic and Medicine
Though it may not be our name on the door
Or on the framed piece of paper on the wall
The eyes of the students see no difference
For the children look up to us as well
And bestow upon us the sacred name of teacher

They know no difference
Until you point it out

Silence is a Luxury

Silence is a luxury so few and far between
Lacking absolute
Resolute in desire
Wanting the lack of
Constant stimulation

Even in rest
We are unable to escape
The noise of a refrigerator
The sound of a ticking clock
A gust of wind

Silence absolute is a dish rarely tasted
If ever

To See You Here

To see you here would have torn my heart to shreds again. That cold chill that used to climb my neck when you were around never sat well with me. Will this horse take me to where it is dark and there is no guidance?

I did that once. I sat upon a hoodoo in Alberta. They don't let you sit there anymore, and that is probably for the best. There were snakes all around me as the sun and the heat of the summer began to take my mind and bend it, twist and shape it to fit around the curvature of the undulating rock upon which I sat. I watched as the world around me began to change colour and suddenly took a sharp turn to the left. I heard an eagle scream, but it could have been me. I am not sure.

I felt alone, unknown and unwanted, with overwhelming feelings. I was alone, alone in the desert, lost like a small child in this wilderness somewhat familiar. It took some time to know that I was safe, but I still felt vacant, empty, like there had been a death in the family, like the death of a brother, ostracized and estranged, the black sheep in a field of grey ones who were trying their best to be snow white. Did I even have a brother? I wonder about this often. Would he have picked me up when I was down?

I can start to see green out of the window, the first budding leaves of a spring so badly needed, desperately, passionately desired, like a long-lost lover, a soldier home from war. It is medicine, mother's milk for the damned, the udder of a dairy cow, engorged and swollen, needing to be emptied, lest the milk go to waste and the cow dries up.

At least, that's how I think it works. What do I know? I'm a city kid.

Did You Walk Through Fire

Did you walk through fire to get here?
I know a much easier way
The scenery may not be as pleasant,
But at least it saves the pain

The Windows Rattle

The windows rattle as the wind blows
I can feel the building sway
In my hotel room in Saskatoon
Up on the 8th floor

I look out the window at 1:00 AM
I watch the city workers
Good Union staff,
Clean the streets while others sleep

The South Saskatchewan River
Flows east below me
Underneath the many bridges of Saskatoon
City lights glimmer
Reflected off the moving water
Flashes of orange in the black water

My Uncle Ivan died in this river so very long ago
A few months after my dad died
I was just a child

I can never look at it
As just a river

Winds Blow Change

Winds blow change from unexpected directions
Superseding what you thought you knew
Reality rattled
But not completely shattered
Baby steps to the very edge of what you assumed you knew

One never really knows how little they know
Until they are asked a question
And they haven't got a clue about the answer

Savant in one way
Newborn baby in another
Hoping like hell that the paths cross somewhere

Lauded as a child for having your nose in a book
Called smart, built-up self-esteem
Your herd got away from you when
Push came to shove
It shook the pedestal you felt they put you on,
When they asked you a question
And you didn't know the answer

Memory: A Noun

Memory, a noun

The place I go back to
When where I am is not so sweet

Memory, a place

Young boy standing on a sidewalk
Staring down where the snow melted
Gravel and dirt
Scattered into the verge
Where grass meets concrete
Garbage scattered 'round the bases of caragana hedges
Ground once buried under snow now bare
Wind, warm and cold at the same time
Blowing the scent of spring around the city

Memory, a time

Dusk and headlights
Summer evening on the same sidewalk
Young boy now a young man
Aching for a good time
Looking for a place to be
Seeking noise and excitement
His high-top shoes scuffed

Stolen from a boot rack at a high school
They will carry him all night

Searching for something,
A vague idea of what he's looking for
Something he cannot fully articulate
The closest approximation is the feeling he got
Standing on the midway late on a Friday night
Looking at the lights

Memory, a man

The colour grey creeping into thinning hair
He looks down on the sidewalk
Past his body, gone to fat
The lean figure of his youth vanished forever
Remembering the last time he stood at this place
Now feeling sorry for himself
Lamenting the loss of how he once looked and felt
Wishing he could go back
Perhaps conveniently forgetting the deprivation
which brought him the lean body
He finds it funny, nostalgia has a way
Of omitting the bad times
From time to time
And how memory can be a funny old thing

Once, I Knocked Upon the Door

Once, I knocked upon a door
as I stood in the sleet
I could hear shuffling,
and I wondered,
Were those dogs,
or are they just hiding,
like I would when Jehovah's Witnesses came to the door?

I pounded on the door
The shuffling stopped,
and all was still

"Shh, listen,"
I said to myself, and I
began to count backwards,
"Five, four, three, two, one..."

Now I was beating upon the door,
rap upon rap.
Crack
There went the cheap ring of white gold I used to wear

Ready to kick in the door,
until the lady next door said,
"No one lives there anymore."

What Shade of Brown?

What shade of brown would you rather I be?
You seem so fixated on the lightness of my skin
And how it pertains to my being Indigenous,
Perhaps it's only fair to formally ask you to your face.

What shade of brown would you rather I be?
Is there a particular pigment you have in mind?
I know that you would rather
I was much darker than I am,
Dark like my father, perhaps,
Or at least as coffee brown as my grandmother,
But not like my pale Irish great grandfather, right?
The one who married the *bois-brule* daughter
of a Red River Rebellion veteran.

What shade of brown would you rather I be?
Since you're so keen to focus on my light skin
and how, if I were darker, I might be more Indian
in your eyes, correct?
Dark enough that my life would have been made
a little harder than it was, is that it?
I look at my pale arms, my pale hands.
This light skin didn't keep me from growing up
in a Residential School
This light skin didn't stop the loss of my culture
and my language
This light skin didn't stop the despair and loneliness
of growing up poor
This light skin didn't stop me from being followed
by store security all the time

This light skin didn't stop the fights on the playground,
or the racial slurs hurled at me
This light skin didn't stop the cops from slowing down
whenever they passed me on the street
This light skin didn't stop the high school guidance counselor
from saying that I was going to end up in jail or on drugs
"just like the rest of them."

What shade of brown would you rather I be?
Dark enough so there would be no question, right?
Dark enough so that I didn't have to constantly
justify my heritage,
Not constantly having to lay out my entire family tree
To prove that I am Indigenous,
Like the Germans had to prove their racial purity time and
again to the authorities in the 1930s,
Lest they be sent to the camps,
Blood quantum and all that?

What shade of brown would you rather I be?
I look at my pale arms, my pale hands.
This light skin has brought me dirty looks
on my mother's reserve every time I visit
This light skin has brought me sideways glances in ceremony,
This light skin had people asking in Cree,
"What's that white guy doing here?"
Not knowing that I understood what they were saying.
This light skin has brought the accusations of being a liar,
the double takes when using my Status Card to get gas,
being told I'm not "really Indian,"
being called a "monias" or a "wannabe."

This light skin had people in a store call mall security
because they thought my father was kidnapping me
when I was a child, because I wasn't as dark as him.
This light skin brought me alienation,
ostracism and condemnation
This light skin forever keeps me feeling "less than" and
seemingly on the outside, not really welcome
into the sacred circle, not fully comfortable sharing
my experiences for fear of not being believed.

I'm not going anywhere, so, again, I ask you,
What shade of brown would you rather I be?

By Any Other Name

By any other name
Would you tread so lightly?
Would you be so cautious
If they never knew it was you?

By any other name
Hiding in the shadows,
Would you hold your tongue
or would you speak your piece?

Behind the Curtain

Behind the curtain
Staring out past the stage lights to the
Dark places full of empty seats

Ghosts of lines said long ago
By actors long since gone from
The spotlight

These boards once creaked under my feet
Standing here, pretending to be someone else
Pretending that the audience was not there

Do I miss it?
Life on the road, a moment on stage

Sometimes
But not enough to go back to it
I only miss it enough to pull this old envelope
from my back pocket
and scribble these few lines

Can You See the Light?

Can you see the light?
It's just there
Creeping out from behind the cloud
Or from under the crack of the bedroom door
Long after you were told to go to bed

The light is there on stage
The stage crews use smoke to turn it into
Pillars and columns

Light as I found comforting
A lightbulb burning above a front door
Another lit through a picture window
of a house on the Rez
After you've been driving all night in the winter

There is nothing holy in light
No divine being, no god
It is but a byproduct of fire
Contained or otherwise

But can you see it?

Someone Said Today

Someone said today
That I belong to the
"Cree Race"

Well, madam,
Allow me to educate
As well as disseminate
That which I wish to illuminate
What one they tried to eradicate
Permit me to
Elucidate...

There is no "race."
It is the common shared experience
The unbroken line of
Fifteen thousand years
of my relations
my family
my ancestors
living, thriving, surviving
in the land between
those Great Lakes
and those Rocky Mountains

You see, madam,
it is
Generation after Generation
Surviving these winters
While hunting in those forests
Fishing in those waters

Hunkered down against
Anything the prairie
Or the woodlands
Could throw at us
If there is such a thing as a
"Cree Race", madam,
It would be the race to eliminate
The historical, allegorical and colonial way of thinking
That placed those words into your mind
Upon your tongue
And past your teeth.

My Incantation

My past is just that,
The past

No longer shall I let it dictate to me
No longer shall I let it poison me
No longer shall my past be my life

I do not forgive
But I release it.

Great is the Energy of the Hot Red Light

Great is the energy of the hot red light
Car doors slamming, ring out like gunshots
And the sounds of the birds stop

They say this is my home
Though I've never had feelings that way

Mine is a large family
Peace be unto those whom I will never meet

It's an odd feeling to be well known outside the clan
but unknown within it
Playing endless games of "who's your mom?"
with each person you meet

Big skies and dust covered dashboards
Prefabricated houses and dead cars
Everywhere there are gravel roads and dandelions
and poplar trees
I come here not to visit, but to bury the dead
who lie in state
in the school gym where the funerals are held
And in the Presbyterian church yard
where untold cousins lie buried

Road Cases

I've led a life
You've led a life
We've all led lives
It's what we do

My life is a guitar case,
Battered and scratched as it is

I've played the song and danced
Been the man in the spotlight,
Then the guy operating the spotlight,
Running the microphone cable.

I'm a survivor
But only in the sense that
I'm still here.

I haven't come through unscathed
But so what?
No one has,
Not even you

I wish I had the imagination
To have created this life
Each moment to me is
Like the road cases I used to lug around the country
As a roadie

For the most part,
I try to leave them stacked

in the dark corners of my mind
Rarely open them
Rarely pulling out the contents

There's a few
That will never be opened again,
One or two that have been opened too many times
A couple where I've lost the key, and they will stay locked

There's no rhyme or reason to my stories
They may seem scattered
But it's just how the cases were stacked
If you've moved house as many times as I have
You know that shit tends to get unpacked
In the order in which it sits
While the boxes with the kitchen things
Logically should be unpacked first
If the first box you open contains knick-knacks
Then Goddamnit,
Unpack the knick-knacks.

One bit of advice, though
Never pack the coffee pot
Always make sure
It rides shotgun with you
To the next place

Insomnia Pt. 2

The damnedest things will wake me up in the middle of the night

I'll be warm,
Drifting off under the covers, when
All of a sudden
I'll jump to my feet

Once I eliminated most of those distractions
That invade my mind
I'll climb back into that
Rapidly cooling space between the sheets
Lay my head down upon the pillow
Wide awake for another half hour.

It's as if night slips away on me
It always seemed that way
As long as it is still dark outside
You can bullshit yourself that there is still time
To sneak in a few hours' sleep
Before the sun rises
There was always time for
One more page
One more paragraph.
As long as it was still dark the party could continue
But when the night died
So did the party

Something about stretching that night out
as long as I could

Before the first light of morning
Washed over the trees and the grass outside and
Painted the world a soft blue colour
To mingle with the orange of the streetlights

Then again, there are some nights
When I watch the news or read some online comments
I sit there, staring at the television, numb

I hate when those nights happen

Once It Seems I Was a Giant

Once, it seems,
I was a giant
With long black hair
a bushy beard
long tattooed limbs
I carried forests in my arms
My fists held trees
Branches hung heavy with
Plentiful fruit
Bundles of cut timber
To build scaffolds
Frameworks
My legs were caissons
Sunk deep into the earth
Foundations upon which
Battlements became bridges
Garrisoned with the wise ones
I was skinned in steel
One hundred thousand riveted plates
Impenetrable bulwarks deflecting the cannonballs
Once upon a time
When I was a younger man

Now only the tattoos remain

Life in Dystopia

(Observations on the First Run for Groceries at the start of the Pandemic)

I arrived at 8:00 am. There were already people lined up, waiting for the doors to open to the general public. There are no masks in the crowd. Everyone is barefaced, and their emotions are written upon every line of exposed skin.

The security guard stands at the door, a counter in his hands, clicking as each person steps into the store. I reach for a cart, and I wish for a disinfectant wipe, but there's none. You use your sleeve as much as you can, but it's not practical, so your bare hand touches the shopping cart handle.

I went first to the paper aisle. There was nothing, not a roll of toilet paper to be had. From the looks of it, there haven't been any for days.

As you walk down the aisles, you're beyond aware of everyone around you, and it feels like there are a lot of people there. You suddenly become aware of every breath you're taking, and the paranoia kicks in. "Which breath will it be that gives it to me?"

Social distancing is almost impossible. There is no room in the aisles. You hold your breath and lean away from people as they pass you. You try not to look anyone in the eye, and they're doing the same.

You feel suffocated, so you duck into the organic aisle, because no one is there, just to take a moment.

From somewhere off in the distance, someone coughs, and you grow cold.

The line for the checkout is long. It snakes single file down the dairy aisle, ending near the tank where they keep the live lobsters. You stare at the lobster tank to avoid making eye contact, and you envy the lobsters for their isolation.

You join the queue, trying your very best to maintain distance. The staff are limiting the number of people at the tills, so any forward movement is in increments of inches.

There is more coughing, this time from in front of you, from someone in line ahead of you, in the airspace in which you will find yourself momentarily. I look around. There are way more people in this store than there should be.

I've spent the last seven days safe at home, in the country, far away from it, isolated, keeping myself and my family safe, and weighing heavy upon my mind is the knowledge that I have broken that protective barrier, so that we don't starve.

How I envy those lobsters. At least they are oblivious to their fate.

You Say You Are the Common Man

You say you are the common man
that you try to understand
Asking questions while you can
Hoping some will sit down beside you

You've practiced your soliloquy
Tied yourself against the tree
Thinking that I will agree
even though you're really free
You ask me to come along and untie you

You wear a feather in your hair
You lift your shirt, and under there
A crucifix dangles in the air
You'll have to make up your mind
Are you colonized, or aren't you?

I Keep Tearing at the Edges

I keep tearing at the edges of my tiny victories
Their pages curling from the heat
Sinking deeper in my chair
My polite discourse a wisp of smoke
Or a sip of water which makes me choke
While you are scolding me like a naughty child
For being wild, untamed
Leaving me stinging from the belt

They are old writings,
Words I wrote so long ago
Put far away
Hidden in the shadows where they belong
Full of rotten phrases
Nonsensical meanderings on paper
I was going to save for later
Prose once meant to be a savior
Worthless now like an English Shilling

Rubbed the wrong way
Now here I sit
Staring

What has become of all my work?
The canvas is gone, and the paint dried up
I feel that I have lost the game

I've changed the water,
and the creatures have stopped drinking
The tune has changed,
and the couples have stopped dancing

I want to cry
But what good will it do?
I should write it down
But who will read it?

A pile of paper lies before me
Scribbles dead before they lived
What overdone idea implores me?
I'll walk away until tomorrow

You Call Me From the Water

You call me from the water
And you say you want to follow
And will I come hold your hand

And although the offer is tempting
To push your body under
I'm afraid I must decline

You just can't take the darkness
In the cold and drunken city
And you thought I'd understand

You are your mother's daughter
Bound to break the ice on which you stand
I can give no consolation
I can offer no resilience
I'm a little short this week

And you speak to your god you scream and cry out
On your knees down by my side of the river
With your pockets full of stones

And you are so stoned

I say thank you for calling

I Long for My Wasted Youth

I long for my wasted youth,
For those days when I could be real
How horrible they seemed back then

These winters break me down
I think of warmer places
Somewhere the winds don't blow so cold
and the worst that can happen is a gentle rain

Pinch and pull me in different directions
I thought I was stronger than
This desolation

Learn something new
and you throw me away
Or put me aside until it
Slips from your memory

The day I want it to rain
Only the wind comes to
Blow my topsoil away

From around me
I can hear the wheels turning
I can smell bodies burning
Inside is a yearning
To flee

Your silver lining might be the death of you
I will beat you to death
With your "Have a Nice Day"

A rain delay, brothers and sisters
The philosophical shortcomings of today
As we pick apart your every last decision
So you can question everything you did

They've all gone, now,
They're dying, or they've left me for dead
Abandoned with no formal explanation
A prisoner repeatedly condemned
At least look me in the eye when you lie to me
I can feel the breath leave your lips
As you say you understand
But I can see through your glassy-eyed stare
That this mind that you claim to possess is not there

You say you are the boss
You command me to take a knee
What if I refuse?
Will you put me in chains?
Will you cut off my head?

Am I an outlaw for wanting to be free?

So much to question
Yours is wisdom and time
Whereas mine is a lack thereof
But this is not such a curse
As you might see it

This lack of time leaves little room to learn
My broken innocence all I have
To hold me back
Except you

Impact Upon a Native* Son

** I leave this up to your interpretation*

Impart upon a native son
One born upon the land of his ancestors
Impart upon him the ways of life and harmony
But remember to leave out the bullshit
Passed off as "the way things should be"

Impart upon a native son
That which is whole and true
To love and look after those who walk between
The land beneath his feet and the air above his head

Impart upon a native son
The reasons for each choice
Not for glory or gold
But because it is right

Impart this all upon a native son
For they are old teachings
Stolen long ago
Locked away in sacristies to be forgotten

Impart upon a native son
That which was once forbidden
so that we will forever hold the high ground

You'll Pave the Road for a Pope

You'll pave the road for a pope
As he comes to make his "apology"

You'll pave the road for a pope
But our people cannot drink the water

You'll pave the road for a pope
And use it later to steal our children into foster care

You'll pave the road for a pope
Yet our sisters and mothers continue to vanish

You'll pave the road for a pope
And continue to plunder Mother Earth
for all she is worth to you

You'll pave the road for a pope
And continue to expose us to disease,
continuing to act like everything is normal
As if millions haven't died

You'll pave the road for a pope
While settlers kill us and get away with it

You'll pave the road for a pope
And leave us to suffer yet again

Never Give Me a Headdress

Never give me a headdress
I won't accept it if you do

Every politician has one
Every monied celebrity and so-and-so
You even gave one to the pope
When he was supposed to be here
begging for our forgiveness

Never give me a headdress
Even if you think I've earned it

How long have we fought
The Coachella Princesses and
the Halloween costume stores
The sports fans in Cleveland and Chicago
and Washington DC
Pleading with them to stop wearing them
to concerts and games

Now, we're giving them away like monogrammed pens

Never give me a headdress
For I may be tempted to tear it apart
To take those eagle feathers
To smudge them
And to give them to those more
worthy of holding them
like Newborn babies

after what you've done to them
don't you ever give me a headdress

Where Were You When the Rains Came?

Were you there when the rains came?
The dusty roads made dark
Little craters from each drop
Making mud
Running down the sides of dirty cars
Road dust running like tears through makeup

I watched it drop
I watched it fall, going off like dynamite around me

I took off my shirt and let the cool rain fall upon me
I let my hair out of my braids and
ran my fingers through it
Letting the cold water saturate it
Feeling the cold water run down my back

It hadn't rained in so long; I'd almost forgotten
what it was like
May I never have to live in the desert

The Rain Puddles Here

The rain puddles here
While the mighty rivers of Europe run dry

I never begrudge a rainy day

The green fields of France
and the pastoral lands of England
Parched brown and yellow under heat unknown

The skies above me here, grey as steel
Open over us
The grass soaking my shoes and socks
I value each drop
In honour of those going without

We Shall Learn to Dance Together

We shall learn to dance together
For you are a new partner
And I am still learning your ways

I knew my old partner's steps
Sometimes better than my own
And, while you dance the same
Your steps are much lighter than theirs

While I knew where to place each foot
I am afraid that I will step on your toes from time to time,
and I apologize
It will take some time to get used to, I imagine
But I thank you for dancing with me
until my partner is back on their feet

To the Deer

This heart,
It kept you running for two miles
Through frozen bush and spruce trees
As the sun went down,
Through the darkness, black night
Zigzagging, doubling back on yourself in the snow,
through the willows and over fallen trees,
You ran.
I followed.

For hours in the blowing winter wind
You ran.
I followed.
Into the night
You ran.
I followed.

Sometime this morning,
As dawn broke over that frozen field
Miles from where the bullet struck
This heart stopped beating
And let you rest
As your spirit stepped into the clearing.

I left tobacco in the snow
This offering for you
You made me earn your life
And I thank you for it.

You will feed my family this winter
You will feed the ravens and coyotes
You will feed many

We honour you.

I'm Drinking Too Much Coffee

I'm drinking too much coffee
That can't be good for me
Forsaking sleep to avoid the dreams
That wake me in the night, screaming

Drawing references that only make real sense to me
Drawing inferences that only make sense to me
They break into the bank that is my mind
They break into the vaults inside my mind
They make a mess and tear me up inside
They fill my head with garbage deep inside
One day I'll stop myself and question why
One day I'll stop the world and question why
I cannot let you this far deep inside
I cannot show you all I've tried to hide
A human shield, a father's love denied
Beaten and hit and cursed and chasing a high
This is but a sliver through my eyes
A simple whisper through my
Bloodshot eyes
One day I might unlock the door inside
One day I might decide
But not tonight

You Brought Down the Old Trees

You brought down the old trees
Stripped them of their limbs
Bucked them up in two-foot lengths
Then piled them beside the stump

They were maples and elms
Not indigenous to the place
But they stood for over one hundred years
in the same spot
While the world changed around them

There's very little sawdust on the ground
It's surprising, as it was a big tree
The cement around the stump is clean

My Metis great grandparents planted a tree once,
after they left Red River and Riel
A Manitoba Maple, called *lii zaraab* in Michif
It stood 143 years before they cut it down, too,
But at least it had a ceremony, a funeral of sorts

I bet the exhaust of the chainsaw
Hung in the air for a while,
Along with the loud scream of the two-stroke engines
The smell probably mingled with
the sweet smell of the cut tree

There is sunlight hitting spaces where
it's never really been before

Because the tree cast shade on them
Oh, there was a space there before,
where the sun touched for millions of years
It's still there
But it's under asphalt and cement now

GENELLE AMBER STUDIOS

John Brady McDonald is a Nêhiyawak-Métis writer, artist, historian, musician, playwright, actor and activist born and raised in Prince Albert, Saskatchewan. He is from the Muskeg Lake Cree Nation and the Mistawasis Nêhiyawak. He is the author of several books, and his written works have been published and presented around the globe. *Kitotam*, a poetry collection, was published by Radiant Press in 2021, and *Carrying It Forward*, a book of essays, was published in 2022 and won the Saskatchewan Book Award for Non-fiction and the Indigenous Peoples' Writing Award. He is also an acclaimed public speaker, who has presented in venues across the globe, such as the Ânskohk Aboriginal Literature Festival, the Black Hills Seminars on Reclaiming Youth, the Appalachian Mountain Seminars, the Edmonton and Fort McMurray Literary Festival, the Eden Mills Writers' Festival and the Ottawa International Writers Festival. A noted polymath, John lives in Northern Saskatchewan.